Joseph Haydn
(1732–1809)

Sonatas

Sonates

Sonaten

III

for piano • pour piano • für Klavier

Urtext
K 123

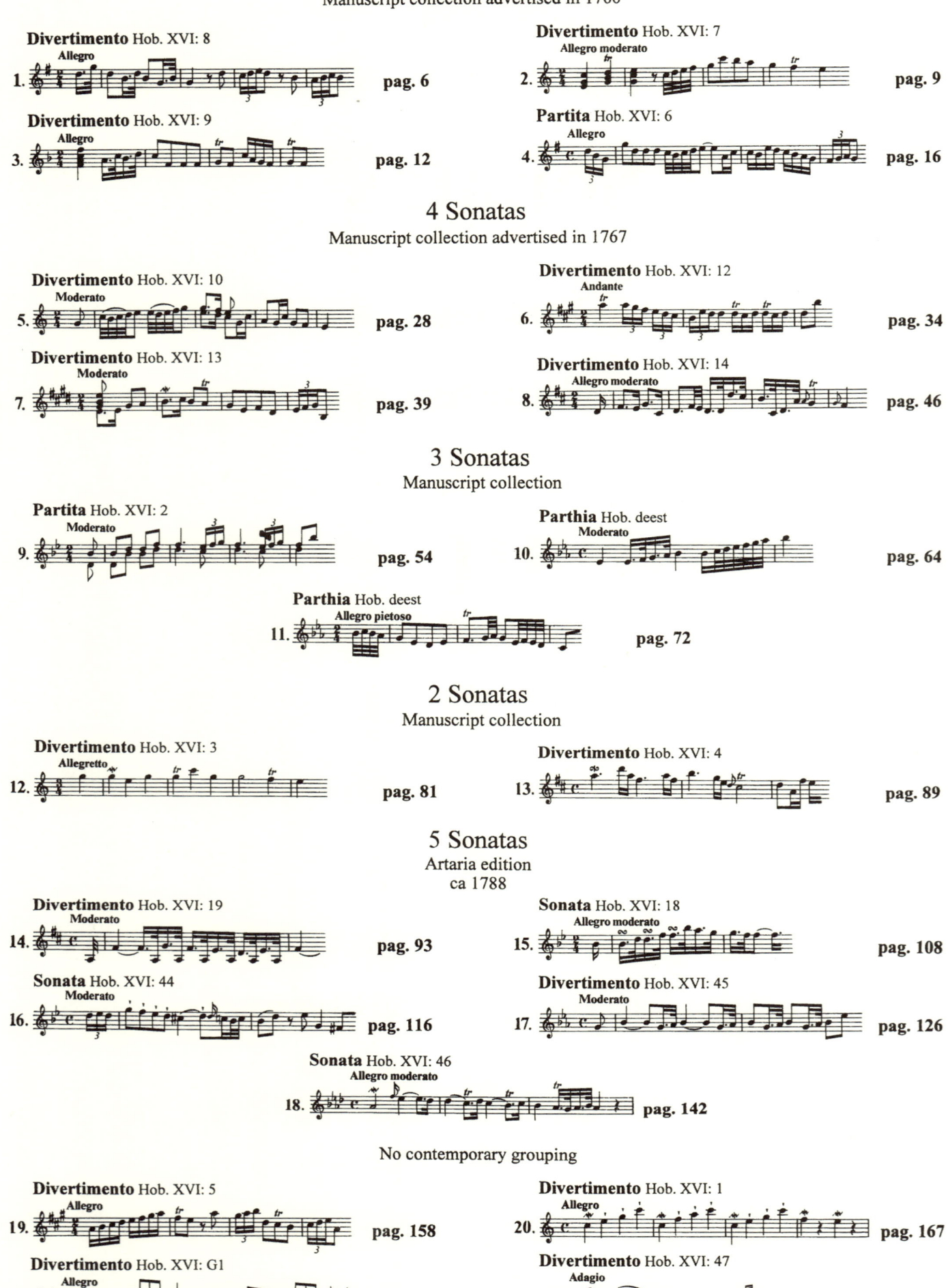

INDEX

II

6 Sonate („Esterházy" Sonate), 1774

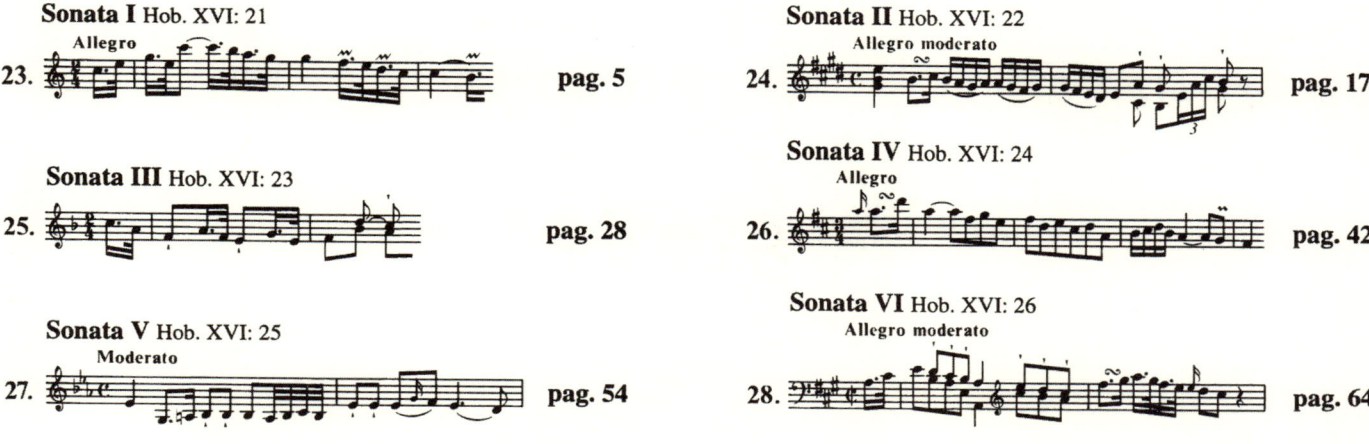

6 Sonate, 1776

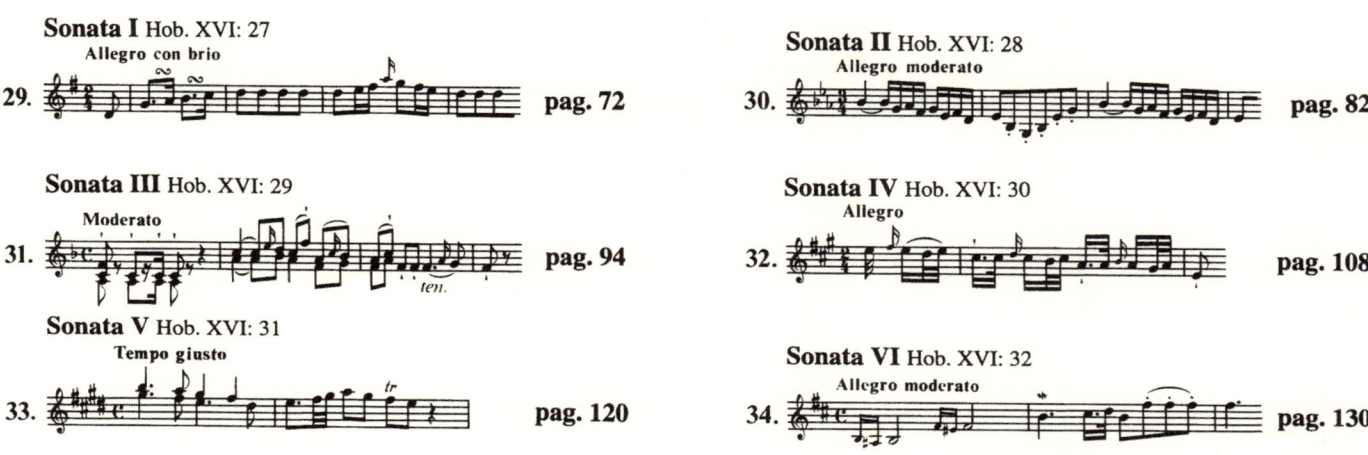

6 Sonate („Auenbrugger" Sonate), 1780

INDEX
III

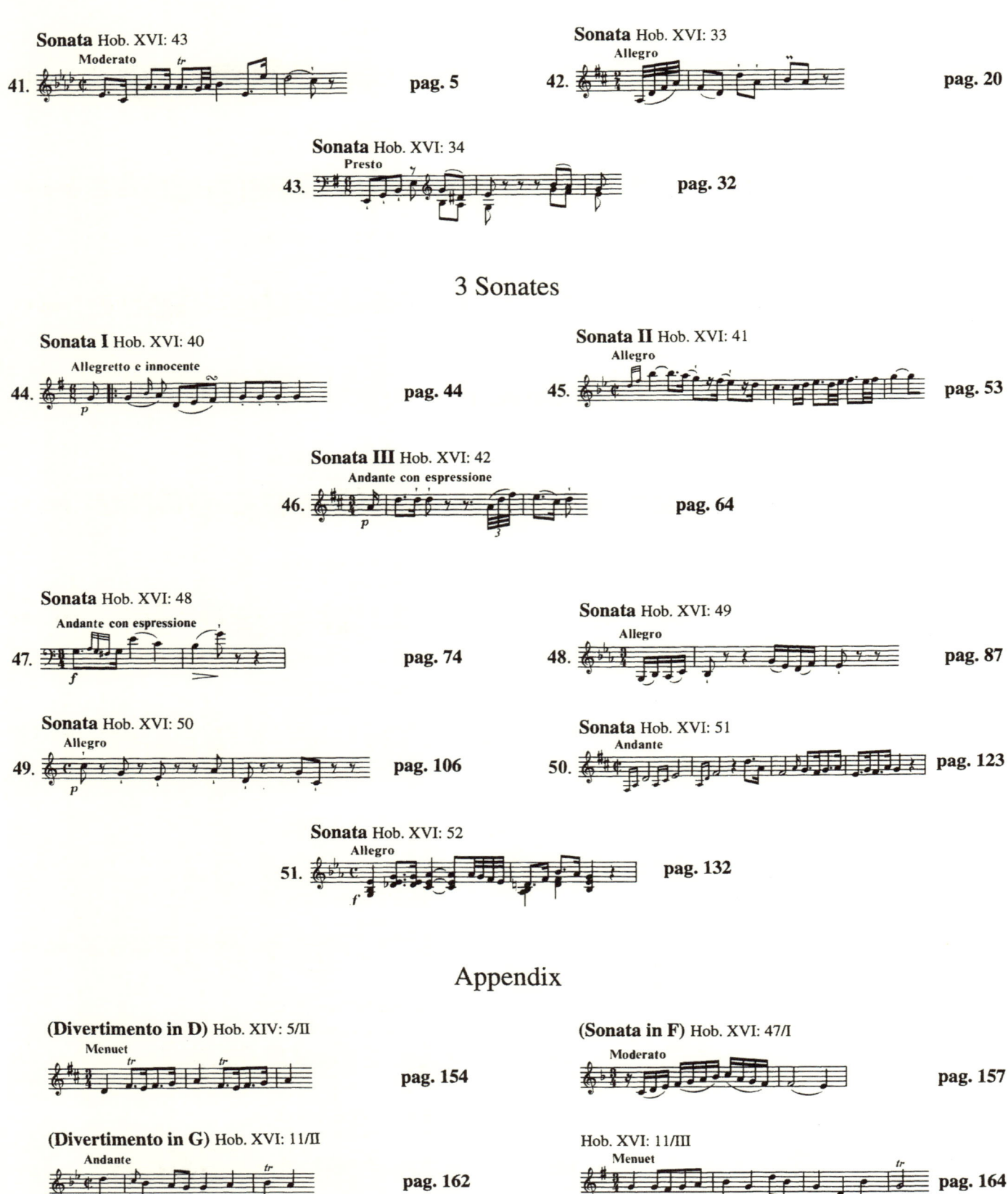

Sonata

Hob. XVI: 43
Published in 1783

Menuetto da Capo

Rondo
Presto

Sonata

Hob. XVI: 33
Published in 1783

Sonata

Hob. XVI: 34
Published in 1783

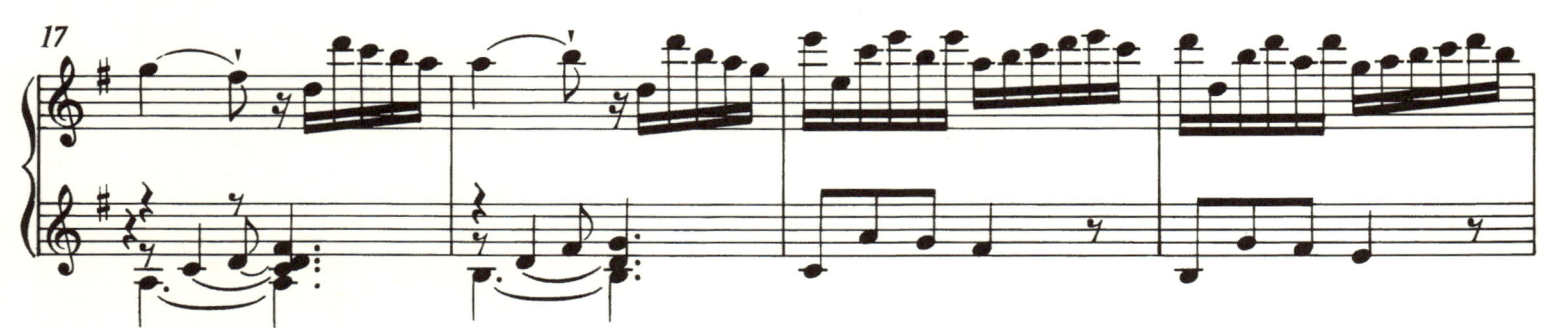

attacca subito

á la Princesse Marie Esterházy

3 Sonates
pour le Pianoforte

Published in 1784

Sonata I

Hob. XVI: 40

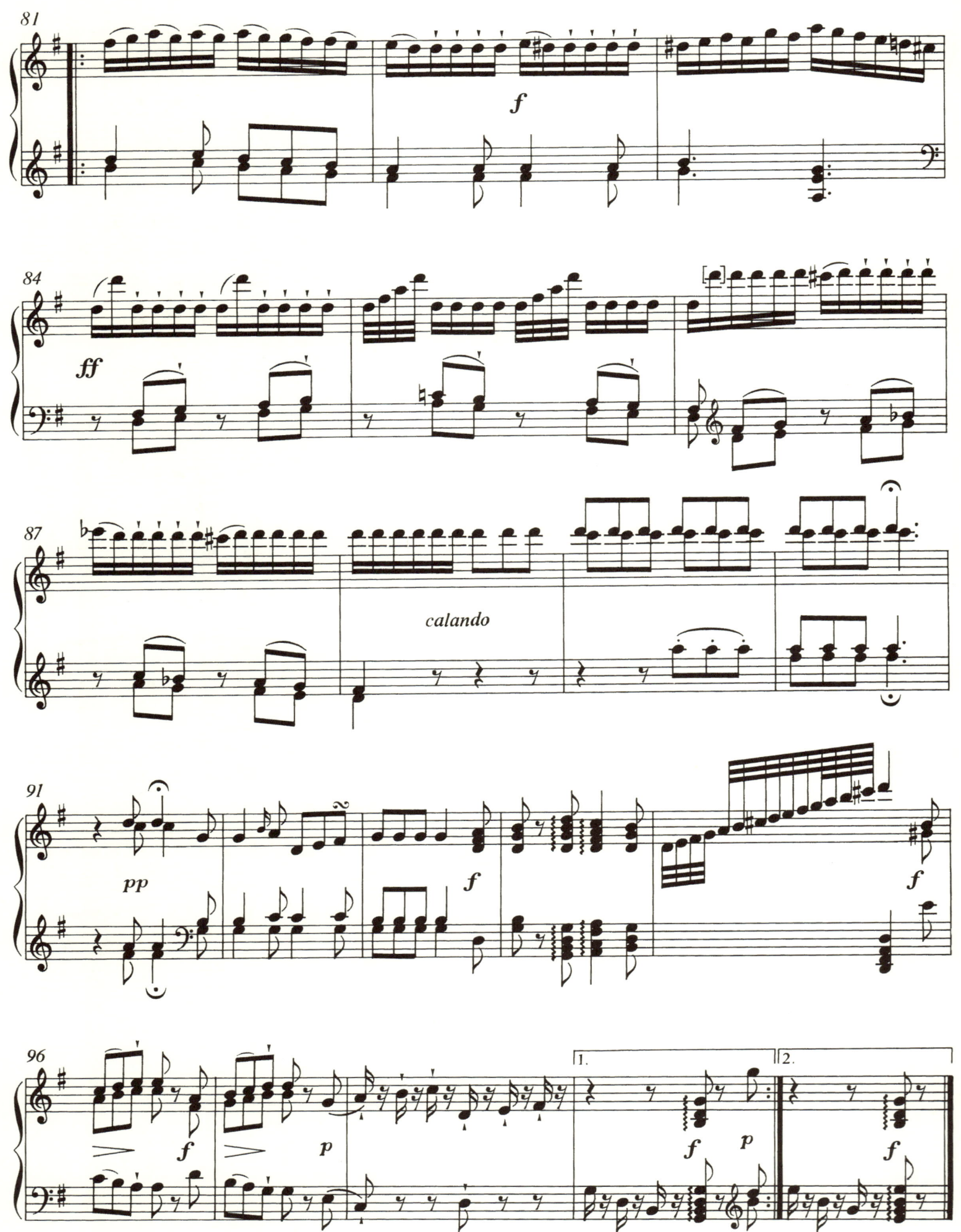

Sonata II

Allegro

Hob. XVI: 41

Sonata III

Hob. XVI: 42

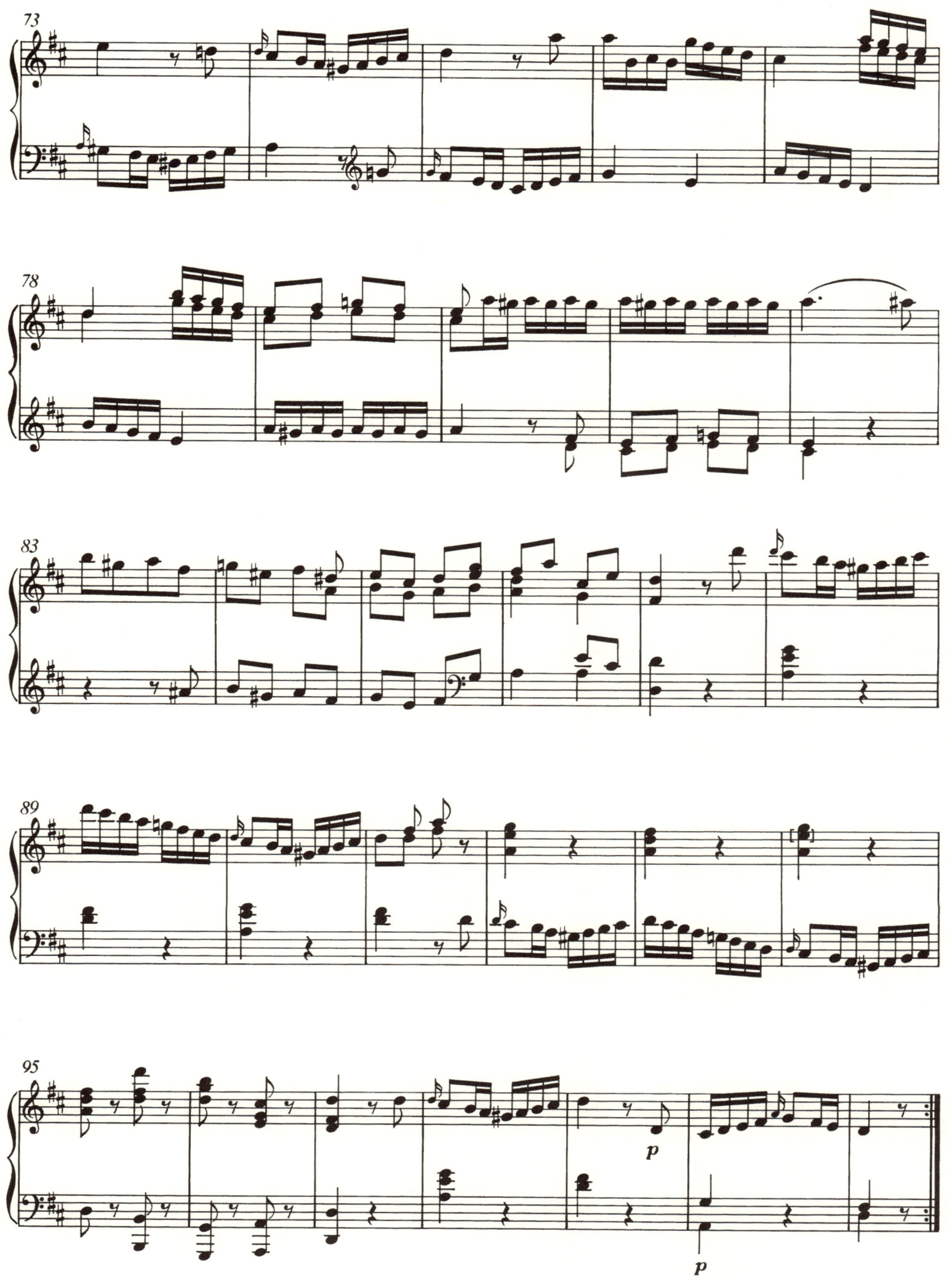

Sonata

Hob. XVI: 48
1789

per Anna da Gerlischek

Sonata
per il Forte-piano

Hob. XVI: 49
1789-1790

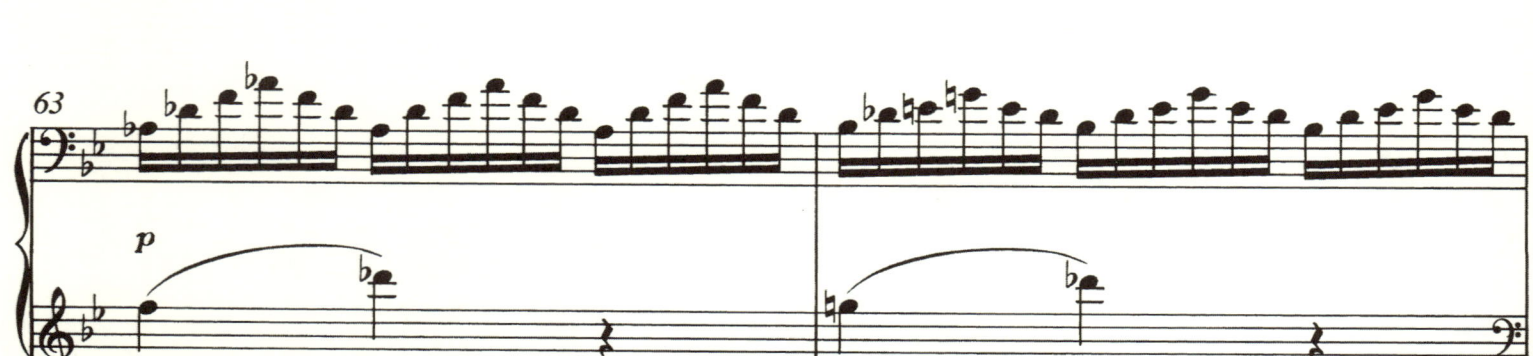

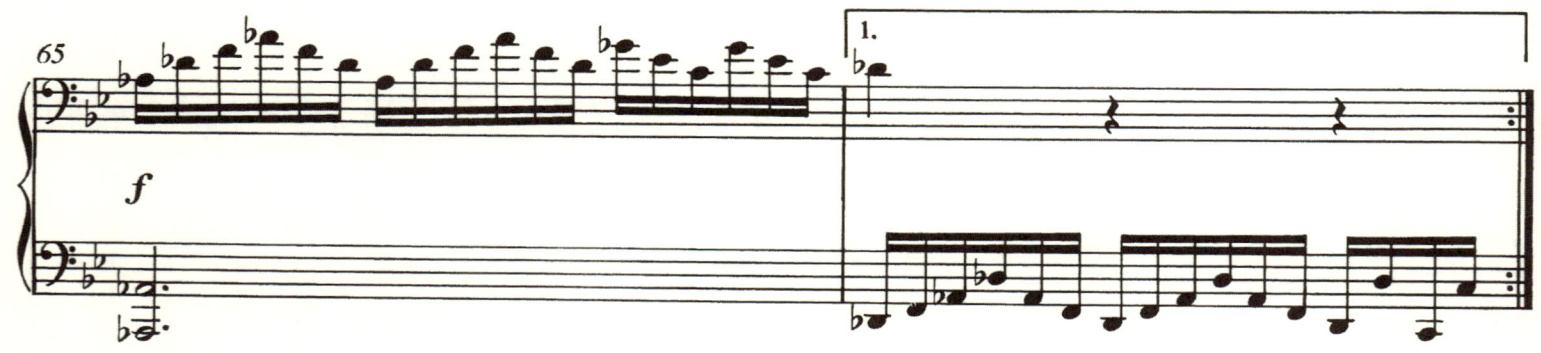

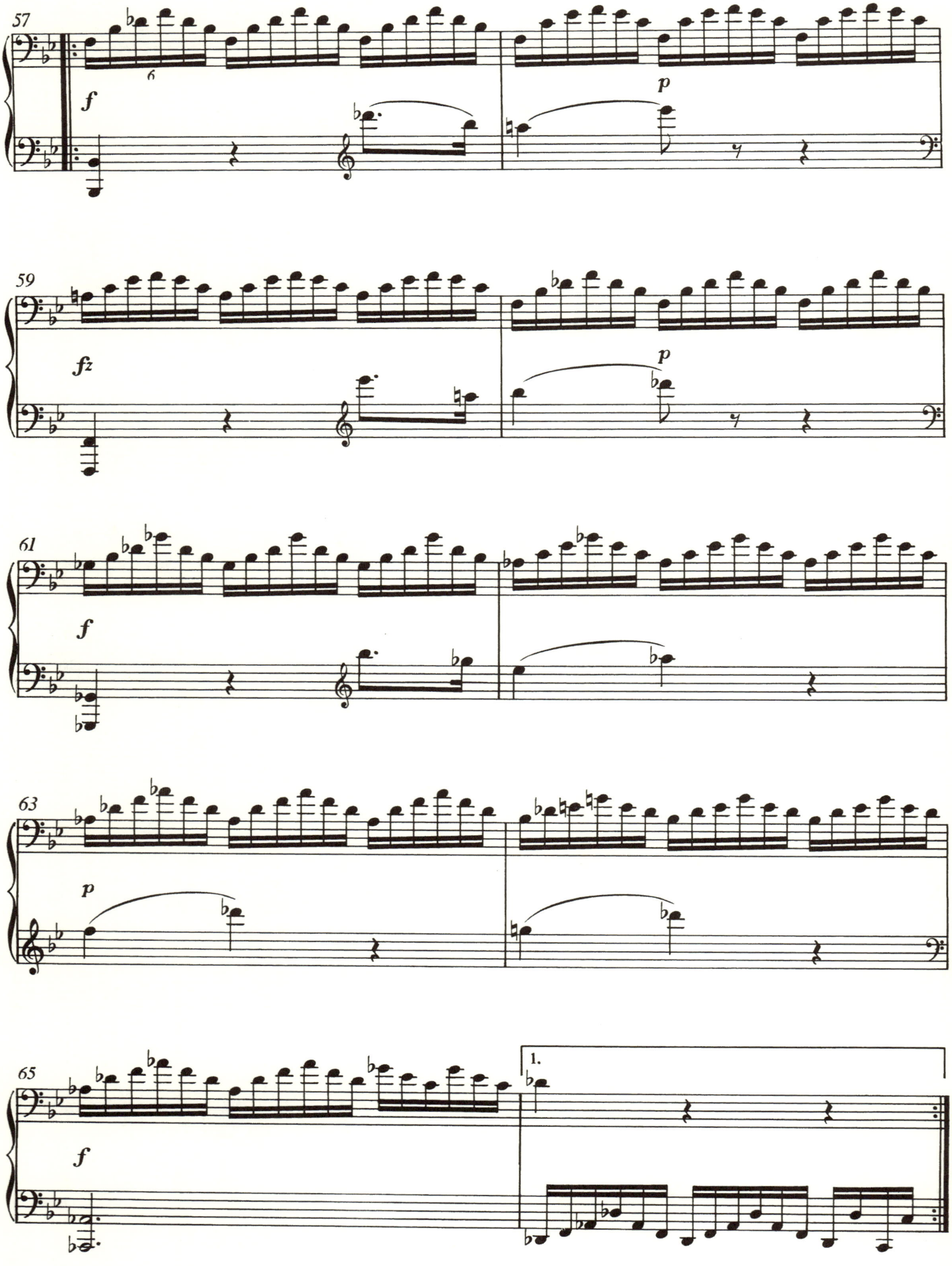
57
6
f
p
59
fz
p
61
f
63
p
65
f
1.

Composed expressly for and dedicated to Mrs Bartolozzi

Grand Sonata
for the Piano Forte

Hob. XVI: 50
Published in 1800

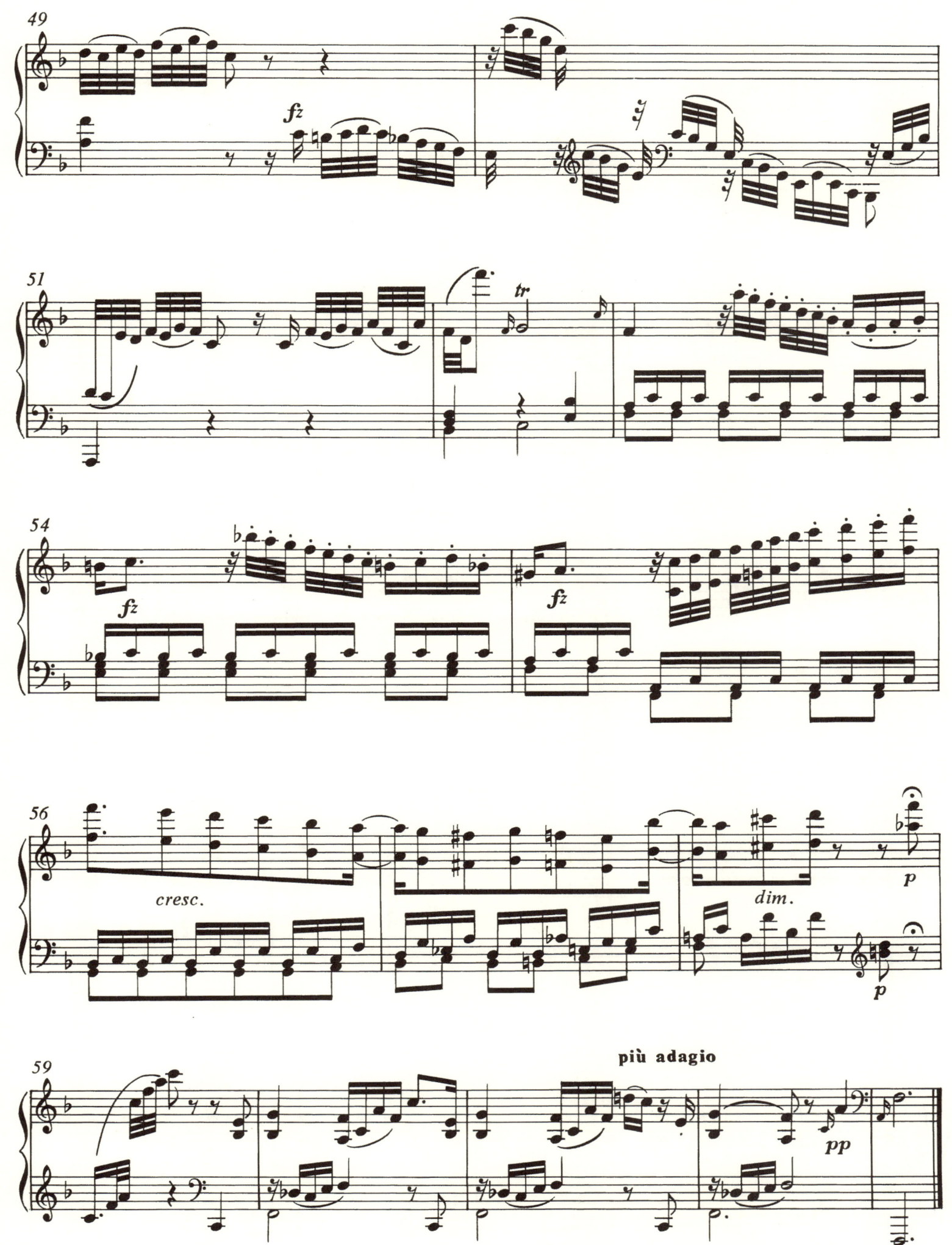

Sonate
pour le Pianoforte

Hob. XVI: 51
Published in 1805

50.

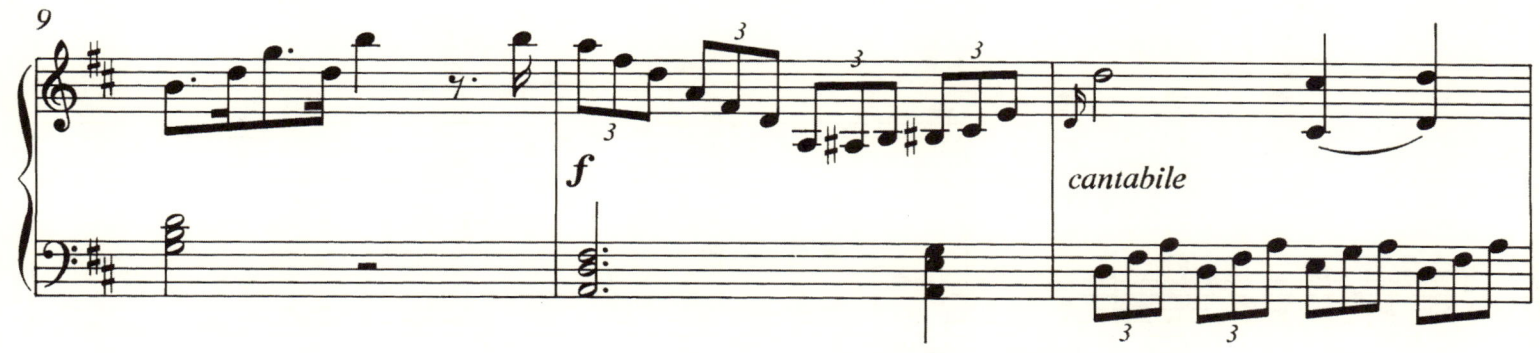

per Teresa da Janson

Sonata

Hob. XVI: 52
1794

51. Allegro

K 123 143

Appendix

(Divertimento in D)

Menuet Hob. XIV: 5/II

Menuet da Capo

(Sonata in F)

Hob. XVI: 47/I

Moderato

(Divertimento in G)

Hob. XVI: 11/II

OVER 25.000 PAGES OF PIANO MUSIC SHEETS ONLINE

K 123

Bach, Beethoven, Brahms, Chopin, Czerny, Debussy, Gershwin, Dvořák, Grieg, Haydn, Joplin, Lyadov, Mendelssohn-Bartholdy, Mozart, Mussorgsky, Purcell, Schubert, Schumann, Scriabin, Tchaikovsky and many more

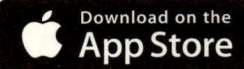

KÖNEMANN

© 2018 koenemann.com GmbH
www.koenemann.com

Editor: Miklós Dolinszky
Responsible co-editor: István Máriássy
Technical editor: Dezső Varga
Engraved by Kottamester Bt., Budapest

ISBN 978-3-7419-1480-5

Printed in China by Reliance Printing

K 123